PARIS

2020

The Food Enthusiast's
Complete Restaurant Guide

Andrew Delaplaine

GET 3 FREE NOVELS
Like political thrillers?
See next page to download 3 FREE page-turning
novels—no strings attached.

I0180645

Andrew Delaplaine is the Food Enthusiast.
When he's not playing tennis,
he dines anonymously
at the Publisher's (sometimes considerable) expense.

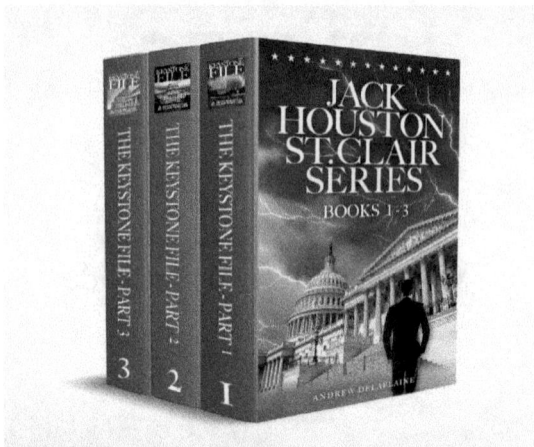

WANT 3 *FREE* THRILLERS?

Why, of course you do!
If you like these writers--
Vince Flynn, Brad Thor, Tom Clancy, James Patterson,
David Baldacci, John Grisham, Brad Meltzer, Daniel
Silva, Don DeLillo
If you like these TV series –
House of Cards, Scandal, West Wing, The Good Wife,
Madam Secretary, Designated Survivor

You'll love the **unputdownable** series about
Jack Houston St. Clair, with political intrigue, romance,
and loads of action and suspense.

Besides writing travel books, I've written political thrillers
for many years that have delighted hundreds of thousands
of readers. I want to introduce you to my work!
Send me an email and I'll send you a link where you can
download the first 3 books in my bestselling series,
absolutely FREE.

Mention **this book** when you email me.
andrewdelaplaine@mac.com

The Food Enthusiast's Complete Restaurant Guide

Table of Contents

INTRODUCTION

Where does one even start?

Yes, it is the most romantic city in the world, to my view. Some think that title belongs to Rome, but for me it will always be Paris.

It doesn't hurt to be in Paris with someone you love. In fact, it makes a discernible difference in your experience there. And while it also helps to be young, that really isn't necessary. It's not essential that you be in love, of course. It's just that there's an added layer of emotion informing everything you see and do, an extra dimension that imbues your time there with an ineffable invisible coating that will fix the time in your memory till the day you die.

I know that sounds a little dramatic, but it's absolutely true. It happened to me. Only once, but it happened.

"You only live once, but if you do it right, once is enough."

Mae West said that.

And before you die, you've got to get to Paris.

At least once.

If it were true that I'd never go back to Paris—I think I'd make a beeline for the Seine, choose one of the lovely classic bridges—and leap to my death in despair.

On a first visit, however, I would recommend walking around a lot at first, just so you get the feel of the city. The sensory impressions you pick up will remain with you forever. Go into a bistro or a bakery and buy some items for a picnic, whether in a park or back at your lodging, overlooking the river, whatever.

Don't visit the churches and museums until *AFTER* your walk around the town, or the section of town you're visiting. They aren't as important as your effort to absorb the city. And I'll tell you from personal experience, those marble floors are *murder* on your feet.

SPEAKING FRENCH

Try to learn a few phrases in French. You can get a little phrasebook anywhere. Just a few words—a greeting, let's say—will go a long way toward defrosting the notably frosty French attitude toward foreigners.

Or just use a translation app on your phone to get a couple of words before you go into a place.

Personally, even though I'm of French ancestry (going back to the 12th Century in La Rochelle and Nantes), my first experiences with the French were just about as unpleasant as others you've heard about.

You don't have to like the people to *accept* them as they are. That was the key to my continuing enjoyment when visiting the country. There are far too many pleasures to absorb in France for you to be put off by the people who happen to live there. I know that statement sounds absurd, but it's not at all.

ARRONDISSEMENT SYSTEM

What are Arrondissements?

Paris is divided into 20 sections or *arrondissements*. Starting in the center of the city, they (very confusingly to newcomers) spiral outwards in a clockwise direction. While the arrondissement system may not help the tourist, each arrondissement has its own character and meaning for the Parisians. Most of the famous tourist attractions can be found in one of the central 8 arrondissements. The last two digits of the postal code denotes the arrondissement (example: the postal code 75001 means the address is located in the 1st arrondissement where you can find the Louvre). On street signs the number of the arrondissement is given in Roman numerals (example: the Eiffel Tower is in the VIIe arrondissement). Here's a list of the 20 arrondissements and some of the more notable attractions to be found in them.

Arrondissement 1 - Louvre

This is the center of Paris and the least populated of the 20 arrondissements. Here you'll find the Louvre Museum, Royal Palace, **Tuileries** gardens, **Forum des Halles**, **Bourse du Commerce** and **Vendôme Square**. The 1st arrondissement includes the western tip of the **Île de la Cité**, the **Sainte-Chapelle** and the **Conciergerie**. Located on the Right Bank (Rive Droit), this area is one of the expensive areas because it's within walking distance to the top tourist destinations and restaurants.

Arrondissement 2 – Bourse

Located on the Right Bank, this is the smallest arrondissement and primarily a business district. Here you'll find the **Palais de la Bourse**, the former stock exchange, the historic National Library and a couple of historic shopping arcades. This is a safe area with affordable accommodations.

Arrondissement 3 – Temple

Also a small arrondissement, this area contains the northern part of the historic **Marais** district that is now a trendy art filled neighborhood. You'll also find the Conservatoire National des Arts et Métiers (National Conservatory of Arts and Crafts), the Picasso Museum and the Carnavalet Museum. This area has a great Jewish quarter with a variety of good restaurants and shops.

Arrondissement 4 - Hôtel-de-Ville

The southern part of the **Marais** district and the eastern part of Île de la Cité, the oldest part of Paris, are located in this arrondissement. Here you'll find the **Île St-Louis** and attractions like **Notre-Dame Cathedral**, the **Place des Vosges**, the city hall, the Gothic Tour St-Jacques and the modern **Centre Pompidou.**

Arrondissement 5 – Panthéon

Located on the Left Bank (Rive Gauche), this area is known as the **Latin Quarter**. Here you'll find the Sorbonne University, the **Panthéon,** the Val-de-Grâce church, the St-Etienne-du-Mont church, the **Cluny Museum**, the Roman-era **Arènes de Lutèce** and the Jardin des Plantes - the city's botanic garden. This area is known as the intellectual center of Paris filled with bohemian restaurants and bookshops.

Arrondissement 6 - Luxembourg

This arrondissement is popular because of the **Jardin du Luxembourg**, one of the world's most popular parks. Here you'll find the **Odéon Theatre**, the **Saint Sulpice** church, and the 11th century Saint-Germain des Prés, the oldest abbey church in Paris. Take a stroll along the famous **boulevard St. Germain** or the rue Jacob where you'll find former homes of famous authors.

Arrondissement 7 - Palais-Bourbon

This is an upscale arrondissement populated with government institutions and major landmarks like the **Eiffel Tower**. Here you'll also find the **Invalides**, **Napoleon's Tomb** and a variety of museums including: the **Musée d'Orsay**, the **Musée Rodin** and the **Musée du Quai Branly**. Other area attractions include: The **Palais Bourbon** (National Assembly), **École Militaire** (Military School) and the UNESCO headquarters.

Arrondissement 8 - Élysée

This arrondissement contains The **Champs-Élysées**, possibly the world's most famous boulevard, and where you'll discover the glamour and elegance of Paris. There a list of must-see attractions like the **Grand Palais**, the Arc de Triumph, and **Petit Palais**, the **Élysée - the Presidential Palace**, the temple-like Madeleine church and Monceau Park. In this district you'll find the famous fashion houses and the elegant hotels and restaurants.

Arrondissement 9 - Opéra

This arrondissement has quite a mixture of areas with the prestigious boulevards n the south and the **Pigalle** area, the old red light district, in the north. Here you'll also find the **Opéra Garnier** - a magnificent opera house, the well-known department store –the **Galeries Lafayette**, and the majestic **Sainte-Trinité** church.

Arrondissement 10 - Enclos-St-Laurent
The **Gare de l'Est** and **Gare du Nord**, two of Paris main railway stations, can be found in this arrondissement. Here you'll find the Canal Saint-Martin with a variety of restaurants and cafes that line its banks. On Saturday afternoons/evenings and all day Sundays, the streets along the canal become car-free zones for cycling and rollerblading. Here you'll also find the neoclassical **Saint-Vincent-de-Paul** church.

Arrondissement 11 - Popincourt
The 11th Arrondissement is mostly residential and is better known for its nightlife than its landmarks. Here you'll find the Cirque d'Hiver, the St. Ambroise church and a nice variety of restaurants. This is a safe area and offers less expensive hotels than the closer arrondissements.

Arrondissement 12 - Reuilly
This arrondissement is most residential but you can find popular attractions like the **Bastille Opera**, the Bercy Stadium and Bercy Park. This area has been revitalized and is popular among the younger crowd who populate the local restaurants, shops and cinemas.

Arrondissement 13 - Gobelins
This mostly residential neighborhood is home to the city's largest **Chinatown**. Landmarks include the National Library and the **Hôpital de la Pitié-Salpêtrière**.

Arrondissement 14 - Observatoire
This is a popular arrondissement for tourists. Attractions include the **Montparnasse Cemetery** and the **Catacombs**. Here you'll also find the Cité Universitaire, and some lovely cafes and restaurants located around the **boulevard du Montparnasse.** The northern tip was home to famous writers like: Hemingway, Henry Miller, F. Scott Fitzgerald, T.S. Eliot, Alice B. Tolkas, and Gertrude Stein.

Arrondissement 15 - Vaugirard
This is largest arrondissement, both in size and population. Here you'll find Tour Maine Montparnasse, the tallest skyscraper in Paris, and the **Parc André Citroën**, one of Paris's most interesting modern parks. This area was home to artists such as Mogdliani, Chagall and Leger.

Arrondissement 16 - Passy
This is the richest arrondissement in the city and only the wealthy are able to afford the rents in this area. Attractions in the arrondissement include the **Palais de Chaillot**, home to several museums and a theatre. Nearby you can find museums like the **Musée Guimet**, with a collection of Asian art, the **Palais de Tokyo**, with exhibitions of modern art, and the Musée

Marmottan, with a collection of impressionist art. This arrondissement boasts a variety of beautiful boulevards, such as the ave d'Iena, ave Foch and ave Victor Hugo as well as the **Bois de Boulogne** Park.

Arrondissement 17 - Batignolles-Monceau
This diverse residential arrondissement features the lowly **Pigalle** neighborhood in the north and the **Palais des Congrès**, a large convention center, at the western tip.

Arrondissement 18 - Butte-Montmartre
This village-like district is a tourist favorite with **Sacré-Coeur** basilica and the **Place du Tertre**. Here you'll find the world famous nightclub **Moulin Rouge**. This area was home to great artists such as Picasso, Matisse, Max Jacob, Utrillo and Renoir. Beware of pickpockets in this area.

Arrondissement 19 - Buttes-Chaumont
This large arrondissement contains one of Paris's most interesting parks, the **Parc des Buttes-Chaumont**. The **Parc de la Villette**, a more modern park in the district, contains the Museum of Science and Industry. Here you'll find some excellent African and Middle Eastern restaurants.

Arrondissement 20 - Ménilmontant
This is a mostly residential arrondissement but it does contain the **Cimetière du Père-Lachaise,** the city's most famous cemetery where famous citizens like Oscar Wilde, Isadora Duncan, Colette, Edith Piaf and Jim Morrison of the Doors are buried.

GETTING ABOUT

UBER

Uber is available and is easy to use. Download the app if you don't already have it and you're all set to go. Especially if you're short on time and don't want to learn the ins and outs of the Metro, this is the best way to get around. Some drivers won't speak much English, but the app tells them where to drop you off.

Get a discount by using my code when you download the App to your phone.
Uber – andrewd145

Paris is made for walking and is a great city to see by foot. This is the only true way to really explore the city. Stroll the streets, meet the people, and enjoy the sights and smells of this colorful city. You'll see something new in almost every block, a Renaissance square, a beautiful cathedral, street vendors, and numerous cafes where you can stop and people watch. **City Discovery** offers **Walking Tours** of the city. www.city-discovery.com

.

THE MÉTRO

Paris has one of the oldest and best systems in the world with approximately 300 stations. Traveling by train is probably the fastest way to get around Paris. You can get within a few blocks of anywhere you want to go in Paris. Each line has a different number and color. The final destinations are clearly marked on subway maps and in the system's underground passageways.

Tickets are sold in the ticket booth in the station (one at a time, ten, or 1 day or multiple days). Métro maps are available at the stations and are posted all over the system. Métro maps are also in most tourist

guidebooks. The Métro runs daily from 5:30 a.m. to 12:40 a.m. (last departure at 1:30 a.m. Fri-Sat). The Métro is reasonably safe but beware of pickpockets. Hold on to your ticket as you sometimes need it to change trains or to exit. www.parismetro.com

THE RER TRAIN

The RER (**Réseau Express Regional**) is a suburban train system that passes through the heart of the city. Faster than the Metro, this train runs daily from 5 a.m. to 1 a.m. The difference is there are five express lines that connect Paris to the surrounding suburbs with several stops in central Paris. Your Metro ticket is good on this train, but only in the central part of the city, you'll need a separate RER ticket if you're traveling to the suburbs.

BUS

Buses are a slower alternative to the Métro. Most buses run from 6:30 a.m. to 9:30 a.m. with limited service on Sundays and holidays. Use your Métro tickets or buy tickets directly from the driver. Maps of the bus routes can be found at the bus stops. Maps list all the stops, highlights, and your current location. Each bus has a different number and corresponding color. At night, after the bus and Métro services stop running, you can travel on one of the night bus lines known as

Noctilien

https://www.ratp.fr/noctiliens

Mon-Thurs every hour 12:30 a.m.-5:30 a.m.; Fri-Sat every 30 minutes.

Most of these buses leave from Place du Châtelet and cross the city's major streets before leaving Paris for the suburbs.

TRAM

Paris has three tramway lines: Line 1 runs from Saint-Denis RER station to Noisy-le-Sec; Line 2 runs from La Défense to Porte de Versailles-Parc des expositions; and Line 3 from Pont du Garigliano to Porte d'Ivry. These lines connect to bus stops and Métro and RER stations. Tickets are the same price as the Métro but are not often used by tourists as they run along the outskirts of Paris. www.tram-idf.fr

TAXIS

Traveling the city by taxi is quite easy since there are nearly 15,000 taxis in Paris and taxi stands all over the city. If the taxi light is on you can even hail one in the street, if the light is dim that means it's occupied. Taxis are fairly inexpensive and it's often the easiest way to get back to the hotel after a day of sightseeing. Hotel concierges will call you a taxi if you don't want to try your luck on the streets but after you've hailed your first cab you'll feel like a pro. Another option is the 2CV (the Citroën 2CV), compared to the gondolas of Venice. These cars can be booked for tours where you get a private and knowledgeable chauffeur who will take you on a tour of Paris, stop for photos, recommend restaurants, and go where you wish. Yet another option is the **Tuk Tuk**, a three-wheeled open-air vehicle. These cars offer a variety of tours of Paris from the conventional tour to the offbeat tours, all with a friendly local guide.

BOAT

The **Batobus**, a150-passenger glass-topped boat, is an economical way to see Paris. The Batobus travels up and down the Seine and stops at the Champs Elysées, Louvre, Eiffel Tower, Musée d'Orsay, Hôtel de Ville, Saint-Germain-des-Prés, Notre Dame, and Jardin des Plantes. You can jump on and off whenever you feel like it. Of course, don't take the boat if you're

in a hurry but it's a beautiful way to see the city, day or night. The only fares available are day passes (allowing you to get off or on as many times as you wish). Boats come every 15 or 20 minutes, timetable changes every season so check the website.
www.batobus.com

DRIVING

If you drive your car to Paris it's highly recommended that you leave your car somewhere on the edge of town. You won't need your car in the city and even if you feel that you do, driving in Paris can be a frightening experience for the uninitiated. Also, parking is difficult unless you happen to be staying at a hotel that has parking. You need a Paris Carte to park on the street since parking meters don't take coins. Even for long trips outside the city it's easier to take the train.

BIKING

Bikes are a great way to get around Paris. **Paris Bicycle** has a great rentals program using three-speed unisex bikes when you can pick at stations all around the city. There are more than 20,000 bicycles available at 1,500 stations and you can pick up a bike at any **Vélib' Station** and return it to any other. The machines take major credit cards but make sure you press the English language option before you read the instructions. If you're interested in cycling the countryside outside of the city, it's best to rent a bike at your destination. Bike rentals are available at many train stations. For information on cycling in Paris, visit www.ffct.org. Bike tours of Paris with tour guides are also available. Be cautious if you do not know the streets of Paris and remember to cycle on the right-hand side of the street.

VESPAS

A fun way to travel the streets of Paris is on one of the vintage Vespas available for rent from **Left Bank Scooters** (www.leftbankscooters.com).

SEGWAY

Most cities are now offering Segway travel. If you've never used a Segway before it will only take ten minutes or so to master the two-wheel vehicle. The Segway is a fun way to get around Paris. There are also Segway Tours available at **City Discovery** (www.city-discovery.com)

HORSE AND CARRIAGE

For those looking for a romantic Paris experience, try traveling by Horse and Carriage. The carriage can hold up to 4 adults or 2 adults and 3 children. Take the one-hour tour and visit the Eiffel Tower, Champs de Mars, Pont Alexander III, Grand Palais, Champs-Elysees, Arc de Triomphe, and Trocadero. Book through your hotel (hotel pickup and drop off available) or find the carriages parked near the Eiffel Tower.

A TO Z LISTINGS

Ridiculously Extravagant
Sensible Alternatives
Quality Bargain Spots

DID YOU FIND AN INTERESTING PLACE?
If you discover a place you think I should check out
on my next visit, drop me a line, will you? I'll
mention your name if I end up listing it.
andrewdelaplaine@mac.com

ASTIER
44 rue Jean Pierre Timbaud, Paris, +33 1 43 57 16 35
www.restaurant-astier.com

CUISINE: French
DRINKS: Full Bar
SERVING: Lunch & Dinner
PRICE RANGE: $$$
ARRONDISSEMENT: 11th
Authentic Parisian bistro experience here with a great menu of favorites like Beef Bourguignonne and Pork Shoulder. Nice prix fixe option. Unique but tasty desserts.

AU PASSAGE
1bis Passage Saint-Sébastien, Paris, +33 1 43 55 07 52
www.restaurant-aupassage.fr
CUISINE: Modern European, Tapas
DRINKS: Full Bar
SERVING: Lunch, Dinner
PRICE RANGE: $$
ARRONDISSEMENT: 11th
This reinvented neighborhood eatery boasts a serious foodie menu. Menu changes daily. Menu favorites include tapas favorites like: house-made patés and Seafood carpaccio. Excellent wine list. Reservations recommended.

AU PERE TRANQUILLE
16 rue Pierre Lescot, Paris, +33 1 45 08 00 34
No Website, try Facebook
CUISINE: French
DRINKS: Full Bar
SERVING: Breakfast, Lunch and Dinner
PRICE RANGE: $$
ARRONDISSEMENT: 1st

Between the Pompidou Center and Les Halles is this friendly restaurant / bar with a simple menu of salads, crunches and deli meats. Great burgers. Menu in English & French. Café seating outside. There's a quiet upstairs room if you want to avoid the crush downstairs.

AU PIED DE COCHON
6 rue Coquillière, Paris, +33 1 40 13 77 00
www.pieddecochon.com
CUISINE: French/Seafood
DRINKS: Full Bar
SERVING: Open 24 hours
PRICE RANGE: $$$
ARRONDISSEMENT: 1st
Classic Paris eatery (since 1947) with an extensive menu. Lots of café tables lining the street outside. 'Pied de Cochon' means the 'feet of the pig' and here you'll be able to sample many different parts of the pig – the leg, the ears, the tail, etc. My Favorites: Beef tartar; Oysters and other shellfish from Brittany; Onion soup (it's really good here); Crispy pig feet; Veal kidneys flamed with Cognac. You get pig-shaped macarons at the end of the meal. French & English menu.

AUX BONS CRUS
54 Rue Godefroy Cavaignac, Paris, +33 1 45 67 21 13
www.auxbonscrus.fr
CUISINE: French Bistro
DRINKS: Beer & Wine
SERVING: Lunch & Dinner; Closed Sundays
PRICE RANGE: $$
ARRONDISSEMENT: 11th
A true Parisian bistro, this quaint eatery with its red-and-white checked tablecloths offers a menu of family recipes from the region of Lyon, which in my opinion has the absolutely best cuisine in all of France (but everybody their own favorite regional cuisine). New menu comes out weekly. Favorites: try the Terrine du Moment (changes every couple of days); Cod with butter sauce; Quenelles comme a

Lyon; and Pepper steak & fries. Popular with young locals. Reservations recommended.

AUX DEUX AMIS
45 rue Oberkampf, Paris, +33 1 58 30 38 13
No Website
CUISINE: French
DRINKS: Beer & wine only
SERVING: Lunch, Dinner
PRICE RANGE: $$
ARRONDISSEMENT: 11th
This popular restaurant with its copper-topped bar only has a few tables so make reservations if you want to dine here. Menu filled with tapas-style dishes: Tortilla de Janine – acorn-fed ham with grilled almonds and Cheval tartar mixed with raw quail egg. Hip décor and clientele. Wine list of all "natural"

wines, focusing mainly on Burgundy, the Loire and points further south. A really fun place with a sort of divey atmosphere.

BISTRO BELHARA
23 rue Duvivier, Paris, +33 1 45 51 41 77
www.bistrotbelhara.com
CUISINE: French/Bistro
DRINKS: Beer & Wine
SERVING: Lunch & Dinner Tues - Sat; closed Sun & Mon
PRICE RANGE: $$$
ARRONDISSEMENT: 7th
French bistro with an impressive menu, heavily influenced by the cuisine of southwestern France, since the owner is from the Basque region. Fixed menu but you can order substitutions. My Favorites: Pork feet; paté chaud (lovely duck hash & foie gras in flaky pastry); Veal sweetbreads with ham from Bayonne; and, simple as it sounds, a wonderful Chicken with mashed potatoes. You must try the soufflé with a raspberry crème sauce. If you don't want to be that extravagant, get the delectable rice pudding.

BOUILLON JULIEN
16 rue du Faubourg Saint-Denis, *Paris, +33 1 47 70 12 06*
www.bouillon-julien.com
CUISINE: French
DRINKS: Beer & Wine Only
SERVING: Lunch & Dinner
PRICE RANGE: $-$$
ARRONDISSEMENT: 10th
Brasserie-style Art Nouveau eatery offering an updated "old" concept when there were hundreds of bouillons in Paris. (The word "bouillon" means "to boil," but in the 19th century, little restaurants popped up by the hundreds that served workers a soup or stew, broth with some meat—the variations were endless. The concept has been revived and expanded upon.) This is a particularly lovely room, a former brasserie, with a mahogany bar with pewter trimming

designed by famed Art Nouveau artist, Louis Majorell. Take a minute to enjoy the stained glass designed by Louis Trezel. Favorites: the Dorade plate (such a great fish item); and Gaspacho Andalou. Nice selection of French desserts. One of the most beautiful restaurants in Paris. You can reserve here, and thus escape the lines that form up.

BOUILLON PIGALLE
22 boulevard de Clichy, Paris, +33 1 42 59 69 31
www.bouillonpigalle.com
CUISINE: French
DRINKS: Full Bar

SERVING: Lunch & Dinner
PRICE RANGE: $$
ARRONDISSEMENT: 18th
Trendy eatery in the rapidly gentrifying old red light district of Pigalle that packs them in on two levels (the place is vast, always busy) offering a simple menu and whimsical cocktails. Menu is small – mostly cold meats and local dishes designed to share. Delicious eggs mayonnaise, veal blanquette. DJ nights. Nice selection of wines. Come early to avoid the line, and trust me, there will be a line.

BRASSERIE FLO
7 Cour des Petites Ecuries, Paris, +33 1 47 70 13 59
www.floderer-paris.com
CUISINE: Brasseries
DRINKS: Full Bar
SERVING: Lunch & Dinner
PRICE RANGE: $$$
ARRONDISSEMENT: 10th
Typical Brasserie menu but everything here is good. It's been this good for almost a century, boasting a plush décor, brass fittings, dark wood paneling, paintings on the walls, lots of crystal and white tablecloths, crack waiters, enticing atmosphere. My Favorites: Oysters, Duck and Norwegian salmon. Delicious Crème Brûlée is a bit hit here.

BRASSERIE LA MASCOTTE
52 rue des Abbesses, Paris, +33 1 46 06 28 15
www.la-mascotte-montmartre.com
CUISINE: Brasserie
DRINKS: Beer & Wine

SERVING: Breakfast, Lunch & Dinner
PRICE RANGE: $$$
ARRONDISSEMENT: 18th
At the base of one of the many stairs leading up to
Montmartre is this great spot for real Parisian
atmosphere attracting both locals and tourists (but
thankfully more locals than tourists, as it's just off the
path for most tourists). Traditional French menu with
a seafood focus. One of the best raw bars in Paris.
The waiters are effortlessly smooth. My Favorites:
Steak tartar and Oysters. Nice wine list.

BUFFET
8 Rue de la Main d'Or, Paris, +33 1 83 89 63 82
www.restaurantbuffet.fr
CUISINE: French
DRINKS: Full Bar
SERVING: Lunch, Dinner, & Late Night (but closed
Sunday & Monday)
PRICE RANGE: $
ARRONDISSEMENT: 11th
Despite the name, there's no buffet but a short menu
offering modern dishes, not so much traditional, all
written on the blackboard (that changes daily). The
broken tiled-floor and simple wooden tables make the
place ultra-casual. Favorites: Lamb shoulder with
prunes and Lemon sole with hand-cut chips. Limited
wine by the glass list. Reservations recommended.

CAFÉ DES ABATTOIRS
10 rue Gomboust, Paris, +33 1 76 21 77 60
www.cafedesabattoirs.com
CUISINE: French/Barbeque

DRINKS: Full Bar
SERVING: Lunch & Dinner;
PRICE RANGE: $$$
ARRONDISSEMENT: 1st

Chefs not only in Paris but just about everywhere else I travel that have any pretention to hipness or the current trends (places like Portland) are ever-so-quick to boast about their emphasis on vegetables and farm-to-table menus. One begins to wonder if there's a place anymore for a meat & potatoes joint. Near the Place du Marché St-Honoré is this wonderful statement to the contrary run by the Rostang sisters, scions of a great-grandfather, who had a hotel-café with the same name. (They have the Art Deco sign he used—it now hangs here. Wood tables, antique flatware, waiters hurrying past you the way they would at any busy bistro—all of it has a delightfully retro feel. This is not to mean they haven't kept up to date with current demands for quality—their suppliers are top-notch—lamb from Limousin, pork from Terroirs d'Avenir, fowl from Le Coq St-Honoré. They offer set menus with options for main course. My Favorites: Angus Beef Ribs; Baby chicken with a Dijon crust; Lobster swimming in herbed butter; Skirt Steak. Mains come in cast-iron skillets, aromatic and hot. Nice selection of desserts. Reservations recommended.

CAFÉ DU COIN

9 Rue Camille Desmoulins, Paris, +33 01 48 04 82 46
No Website
CUISINE: French/Wine Bar
DRINKS: Wine
SERVING: Breakfast, Lunch, & Dinner
PRICE RANGE: $
ARRONDISSEMENT: 11th

Trendy young people flock here for its simple menu with a great 3-course prix fixe lunch menu. Dinner menu features no main courses, just miniature pizzas (called a pizzette), charcuterie, and cheeses. Reservations necessary for lunch but not accepted for evenings, when the menu shifts from the prix fixe to a la carte tapas-style plates, all of which are utterly delicious. Add this kind of food to a fun atmosphere filled with a bustling crowd and you've got a winner.

CANDELARIA

52 rue de Saintonge, Paris, +33 1 42 74 41 28
www.quixotic-projects.com/venue/candelaria
CUISINE: Mexican
DRINKS: Full Bar
SERVING: Brunch, Lunch, Dinner
PRICE RANGE: $$
ARRONDISSEMENT: 3rd

Yes, you can find good Mexican cuisine in Paris. This is also a great place for Sunday Brunch with a laid-back vibe. They even have a secret back door. It's casual dining at its best. Menu favorites include: Rajas con queso (sautéed peppers with melted cheese) and Tacos de carnitas (roasted pork). Bar in back features an extensive cocktail menu serving concoctions like the Santa Margarita made with Tequila, agave, hibiscus, vanilla and lime.

CARMEN RAGOSTA

8 rue de la grange au belles, Paris, +33 1 42 49 00 71
www.carmenragosta.com

CUISINE: Italian/Vegetarian
DRINKS: Beer & Wine
SERVING: Lunch; closed Mon & Tues
PRICE RANGE: $$$
ARRONDISSEMENT: 10th
In this boutique featuring handmade clothing, you'll find a restaurant offering vegetarian and vegan fare. You sit at tables up next to the racks while the chef works in a tiny kitchen in the back of the house. Incredible risotto and delicious non-dairy tiramisu. Sometimes open for dinner, but call ahead to make sure.

CHAMPEAUX

@Forum des Halles, 101 rue Berger, La Canopée, Paris, +33 1 53 45 84 50
https://www.restaurant-champeaux.com/en
CUISINE: Brasseries
DRINKS: Full Bar
SERVING: Lunch & Dinner;
PRICE RANGE: $$$
ARRONDISSEMENT: 1st / Les Halles
Elegant, sleek and stylish modern restaurant with an impressive bistro menu by the famed Alain Ducasse. My Favorites: Pasta with black truffles; the usual charcuterie boards; steak tartare; there are 6 soufflés, 3 of which are savory (opt for the lobster) and 3 of which are sweet (get the pistachio with a lovely caramel sauce), but there's also a superior Chocolate soufflé. Excellent wine selection. Reservations recommended.

CHEZ GABRIELLE

7 rue de l'Etoile, Paris, +33 1 43 80 23 01
No website
CUISINE: French
DRINKS: Beer & Wine
SERVING: Lunch & Dinner; closed Sunday
PRICE RANGE: $$$
ARRONDISSEMENT: 17th
Small (and I mean tiny) eatery with a great menu of
French fare. My Favorites: Scallops and Escargots.
Save room for dessert – poached peach with crème
brulee. Reservations recommended.

CHEZ GEORGES

1 rue du Mail, Paris, +33 1 42 60 07 11
No Website
CUISINE: French
DRINKS: Full Bar
SERVING: Lunch & Dinner (but closed between
2:30 & 7); closed Sat & Sun
PRICE RANGE: $$$
ARRONDISSEMENT: 2nd / Bourse
Authentic French eatery located on a back street.
Small restaurant with that lovely buzz you get in a
popular bistro frequented by locals. White tablecloths,
leather banquettes, smart waiters—it's all here. They
really pack them in, so expect to be shoulder-to-
shoulder with the tables on either side of you. My
Favorites: Chicken liver paté; frisée salad with
lardons; Duck breast sauced beautifully. Get the apple
tart for dessert. French speaking staff.

CHEZ JANOU

2 rue Roger Verlomme, Paris, +33 1 42 72 28 41
www.chezjanou.fr
CUISINE: French
DRINKS: Full Bar
SERVING: Lunch & Dinner, Dinner only on Sat & Sun.
PRICE RANGE: $$
ARRONDISSEMENT: 3rd
Friendly bistro (waiters speak enough English to order but not enough for conversation) offering an impressive menu and wine list. My Favorites: Osso Bucco over pasta and Duck Breast. Best dessert is the chocolate mousse.

CLOVER

5 rue Perronet, Paris, +33 1 75 50 00 05
www.clover-paris.com
CUISINE: French
DRINKS: Beer & Wine
SERVING: Lunch &Dinner
PRICE RANGE: $$$$
ARRONDISSEMENT: 7th
Tiny little restaurant (maybe 20 seats) created by chef and restaurateur Jean-Francois Piege and his wife Elodie. Known for their contemporary European cuisine. Open kitchen lets you observe every move they make. My Favorites include: Scallops and Chicken bouillon with toasted Jerusalem artichokes. Impressive wine list.

CLOWN BAR

114 rue Amelot, Paris, +33 1 43 55 87 35

www.clown-bar-paris.com
CUISINE: French/Modern European
DRINKS: Full Bar
SERVING: Lunch & Dinner; closed Mon & Tues
PRICE RANGE: $$$
ARRONDISSEMENT: 11th
Bar/restaurant decorated with colorful clown art and a glass ceiling painted with circus scenes. There's nothing whimsical about the food, however. Popular with Parisians for their modern take of classic French dishes. My Favorites: Squid and Foie gras. Reservations recommended.

DA ROSA
62 rue de Seine, Paris, +33 1 40 51 00 09
www.darosa.fr
CUISINE: French
DRINKS: Beer & Wine Only
SERVING: Lunch, Dinner
PRICE RANGE: $$$
ARRONDISSEMENT: 6th
This little shop offers wine, artisan cured meats, cheeses, dried pasta and condiments. Shop for take-out or dine in. Known for their cured hams from Spain, Italy, and Portugal, all available tapas-style or if you prefer a larger portion with toast and a salad. Menu favorites include: Iberian ham and Risotto.

DAVID TOUTAIN
29 rue Surcouf, Paris, +33 1 45 50 11 10
www.davidtoutain.com
CUISINE: Modern European
DRINKS: Beer & Wine

SERVING: Lunch & Dinner; closed Sat & Sun
PRICE RANGE: $$$$
ARRONDISSEMENT: 7th
Creative and artistic high-end eatery with food executed by one of the most expert chefs working today. Reservations necessary. The Spartan atmosphere is not elegant, but the food sure is. My Favorites: Smoked eel in black sesame purée and Cod with plum and corn. Great wine pairings. Tasting menu is suggested for first timers.

DERRIERE
69 rue des Gravilliers, Paris, +33 1 44 61 91 95
 www.derriere-resto.com
CUISINE: Modern European
DRINKS: Full Bar
SERVING: Lunch & Dinner
PRICE RANGE: $$$
ARRONDISSEMENT: 3rd
Kitschy-retro designed eatery with indoor and outdoor seating attracts a youngish crowd of hipsters. The patio is really nice. Has table tennis. Menu favorites: Eggplant appetizer and Classic roast chicken. Vegetarian selections available. Staff accommodating to non-French speaking tourists.

DU PAIN ET DES IDEES
34 rue Yves Toudic, Paris, +33 1 42 40 44 52
www.dupainetdesidees.com
CUISINE: Bakery/Tea Room
DRINKS: No Booze
SERVING: Breads, Pastries
PRICE RANGE: $$
ARRONDISSEMENT: 10th
Even if you don't eat bread at home, in Paris, you
have to give yourself over to BREAD, because it's
never better than it is here. Famous for their breads,
this bakery has received the Gault-Millau prize for
Best Bakery. (When you visit, pay special attention to
the hand-painted ceiling that goes back to the 1860s.)
Here you'll find a great assortment of breads with
choices like Le Rabelais – pain brioche with saffron,
honey and nuts and banana croissants. Pastries are
stuffed with praline, chocolate, pistachio, and god
knows what else.

GEORGE V
FOUR SEASONS

31 Avenue George V, Paris, +33 1 49 52 70 00
https://www.fourseasons.com/paris/dining/lounges/la_galerie/
CUISINE: Mediterranean
DRINKS: Full Bar
SERVING: Lunch & Dinner
PRICE RANGE: $$$$
ARRONDISSEMENT: 8th

As great at the hotel is, I'm writing about its luxurious bar and excellent service. The "hot chocolate grand cru" is one of the delicacies offered but **Afternoon Tea at George V** is truly an elegant experience. Favorites: Blini with cauliflower cream, salmon & Sologne caviar and Lobster brioche with lemon jelly. Choose from an impressive selection of teas or champagne. Tea is served in the **Galerie**, a grand lounge covered with Flemish tapestries, 19th century furniture and beautiful works of art. Live pianist during afternoon tea. Reservations recommended.

GONTRAN CHERRIER

22 rue Caulaincourt, Paris, +33 1 46 06 82 66
www.gontrancherrierboulanger.com
CUISINE: Bakery
DRINKS: No Booze
SERVING: Breads, Pastries
PRICE RANGE: $$
ARRONDISSEMENT: 18th

I have a thing for the bread shops of Paris. There's no wider (or better) selection in the world. Put together picnics in places like this with food you can take out. Chef Cherrier, author of several books on bread and tartines, offers up a variety of baked goods including whole-grain baguettes, bread with curry and grain, and bread with chickpeas and lemon. Here you'll also find a nice selection of delicious pastries and tartes.

JEANNE A
42 rue Jean-Pierre Timbaud, Paris, +33 1 43 55 09 49
www.jeanne-a-comestibles.com/
CUISINE: French
DRINKS: Wine
SERVING: Lunch, Dinner
PRICE RANGE: $$$
ARRONDISSEMENT: 11th
This eat-in épicerie and wine shop from restaurateur
Frederic Public-School offers a nice menu of food
and wines (eat-in or take-out). Menu favorites
include: Roast Challans chicken and crispy skinned
spit-roasted duck. Also try their great assortment of
farm cheeses and delicious desserts like the apple tart.

KUNITORAYA 2
5 rue Villedo, Paris, +33 1 47 03 07 74
www.kunitoraya.com
CUISINE: Japanese

DRINKS: Beer & Wine
SERVING: Lunch & Dinner, Lunch only on Sunday; closed Mon
PRICE RANGE: $$$
ARRONDISSEMENT: 1st
Behind the Palais Royal's fancy arcades is this Japanese food spot with a focus on Udon and tapas. Great range of dishes and wines in a classic bistro setting. Kitchen accommodating to allergies when possible.

L'AMI JEAN
27 rue Malar, Paris, +33 1 47 05 86 89
www.lamijean.fr
CUISINE: French/Basque
DRINKS: Full Bar
SERVING: Lunch & Dinner; closed Sun & Mon
PRICE RANGE: $$$$

ARRONDISSEMENT: 7th

Great French eatery, but with a tilt toward the Basque country. Arrive early for the 7 p.m. seating to avoid the rush. If you don't speak French order the six-course tasting menu. My Favorites: Pork Terrine; lovely sweetbreads sautéed just perfectly; and Monkfish. Save room for the rice pudding – it's just about the best in Paris. Impressive wine list.

L'AMI LOUIS

32 rue du Vertbois, Paris, +33 1 48 87 77 48
CUISINE: French
DRINKS: Beer & Wine Only
SERVING: Lunch, Dinner
PRICE RANGE: $$$$
ARRONDISSEMENT: 3rd

Very popular in the 1930s, this eatery continues its reputation for serving excellent French cuisine. Menu favorites include: Foie gras and Roast Chicken (the most expensive in Paris). One of the best wine lists in the world. Reservations necessary. (Make sure to call to confirm, otherwise you can lose your reservation with about as much explanation from them as if you were asking about the origins of the universe or the meaning of life.) Still, some people say this is probably the greatest bistro in the whole world. Once you taste their potatoes, their *pommes bearnaises*, you'll agree with them.

L'ATELIER DE JOËL ROBUCHON

Hôtel du Pont Royal, 5 rue de Montalembert, Paris, +33 1 42 22 56 56
www.joel-robuchon.com

CUISINE: French/Modern European
DRINKS: Full Bar
SERVING: Lunch & Dinner
PRICE RANGE: $$$$
ARRONDISSEMENT: 7th

Impressive upscale eatery with the kitchen framed in shiny stainless steel boxes that, combined with the low lighting in the rest of the room really puts the focus on the bustling activity of the kitchen workers. There are seats at the bar overlooking the kitchen (in the style of a sushi counter) that bring you even closer to the kitchen. Try the 10-course tasting menu for a wide range of choices. Note: Menu completely in French. If money isn't an object, this is a must on your visit to Paris.

L'AVANT-COMPTOIR

9 Carrefour de l'Odéon, Paris, +33 1 44 27 07 97
www.hotel-paris-relais-saint-germain.com
CUISINE: French
DRINKS: Beer & Wine Only
SERVING: Lunch, Dinner
PRICE RANGE: $$
ARRONDISSEMENT: 6th

Yves Camdehorde's great little bistro located next door to his more lavish restaurant **Le Comptoir**. This bistro offers crepes and sandwiches during the day and in the evening delicious hors d'oeuvres like fried croquettes stuffed with Iberian ham and Oxtail canapés with horseradish cream. Take note, there are no chairs so you'll dine standing at the bar. Go early, because after 8:30, it's impossibly crowded.

LA BUVETTE
67 rue St-Maur, Paris, +33 9 83 56 94 11
http://www.labuvette.paris
CUISINE: French
DRINKS: Beer & Wine
SERVING: Dinner Wed – Sun, Lunch Sat & Sun;
closed Mon & Tues
PRICE RANGE: $$
ARRONDISSEMENT: 11th
Cute little (and I mean little) eatery & wine bar with
copper-ceiling, a zinc-topped bar with stools on one
side of the narrow space with 3 tables on the other
side; more than likely the owner will wait on you.
Small plates menu, with terrines, snacks, salads,
chorizo sandwich; Galician sardines; charcuterie.
Nice wine selection – primarily French.

LA CAVE DE L'INSOLITE
30 rue de la Folie Méricourt, Paris, +33 1 53 36 08 33
www.lacavedelinsolite.fr

CUISINE: Bistros
DRINKS: Wine
SERVING: Brunch, Lunch, Dinner
PRICE RANGE: $$
ARRONDISSEMENT: 11th
Brothers Axel and Arnaud Baraquin run this wine bar-bistro featuring a tasty comfort food menu compiled by Chef Alessandro Candido. Nice wine selection. Menu favorites include: Oven-roasted Porchetta and Grilled Chicken. Prix-fix menus and Sunday brunch.

LA DAME DE PIC
20 rue du Louvre, Paris, +33 1 42 60 40 40
www.anne-sophie-pic.com
CUISINE: French
DRINKS: Full Bar
SERVING: Lunch & Dinner
PRICE RANGE: $$$$
ARRONDISSEMENT: 1st
Modern take of French cuisine. Servers speak French and English. Menu is prix fixe. Oysters and Farm Lamb. Great upscale dining experience with food created by France's only female 3-star Michelin chef. Reservations recommended.

LA FONTAINE DE MARS
129 rue St-Dominique, Paris, +33 1 47 05 46 44
www.fontainedemars.com
CUISINE: French
DRINKS: Full Bar
SERVING: Lunch & Dinner
PRICE RANGE: $$$

ARRONDISSEMENT: 7th

This classic place—a picture-perfect image of a bistro—has been here since 1908 and after some remodeling is now a beautiful two-level eatery with an impressive menu. The old mosaic floors remind you who long it's been here. My Favorites: Escargot de Bourgogne and Foie Gras. Coq au Vin is the best. Delicious desserts.

LA GRAND COLBERT
2 rue Vivienne, Paris, +33 1 42 86 87 88
www.legrandcolbert.fr
CUISINE: French
DRINKS: Full Bar
SERVING: Lunch, Dinner
PRICE RANGE: $$$
ARRONDISSEMENT: 2nd

This traditional French brasserie serves classic French dishes including foie gras, seafood, veal, duck, beef and chateaubriand. Nice wine list. This place is quite popular among Americans because of the last scene in the film "Something's Got to Give." Menu favorites include: Salmon Tartar and Duck in Peppercorn sauce. For dessert try the Crepes Suzette (filled with booze).

LA MARY CELESTE

1 rue Commines, Paris, +33 1 42 77 98 37
www.lemaryceleste.com
CUISINE: Seafood, Tapas/Small Plates
DRINKS: Full Bar
SERVING: Dinner
PRICE RANGE: $$
ARRONDISSEMENT: 3rd
Chef Haan Palcu-Chang serves a menu of tasty small dishes. Menu favorites include Beef shin Chinese Tacos and kimchi. Creative menu of cocktails like the Yolo (short for "You Only Live Once").

LA PATISSERIE CYRIL LIGNAC

24 rue Paul Bert, Paris, +33 1 55 87 21 40
www.lapatisseriecyrillignac.com
CUISINE: Bakery
DRINKS: No Booze
SERVING: Croissants, Pastries
PRICE RANGE: $$$
ARRONDISSEMENT: 11th
Yet another bakery. I can't get enough of them. This bakery offers a nice assortment of pastries and croissants. Tart flavors include: blackcurrant, blueberry, rum baba, flash bourbon vanilla, raspberry and religious chocolate. Great place for lunch serving salads and sandwiches and lots of pastries. All sandwiches served on fresh baguette. Try the pain au

chocolat (chocolate croissant). Without doubt some of the best croissants in town—they're right by the register. Great variety of cakes.

LA POULE AU POT
9 rue Vauvilliers, Paris, +33 1 42 36 32 96
www.lapouleaupot.com
CUISINE: French
DRINKS: Full Bar
SERVING: Dinner; closed Mon
PRICE RANGE: $$$
ARRONDISSEMENT: 1st
Popular eatery and the food is top-notch. Open until 5 a.m. so you can have a 3-hour dinner and you won't be rushed. Famous for their Henri IV (hen cooked slowly in bouillon, celery, potatoes, carrots) and La Poule au Riz Sauce Supreme (poached hen with rice and cream sauce). Other My Favorites: Escargot and Goat Cheese Crostini. Excellent Crème brûlée.

LA RÉSERVE HOTEL & SPA
42 Avenue Gabriel, Paris, +33 1 58 36 60 60
https://www.lareserve-paris.com/en/
ARRONDISSEMENT: 8th
Set in a 19th-century mansion (originally housing the brother of
Napoleon III, known as the Duc de Morny), this luxury hotel
offers elegantly decorated suites and rooms. This is one of those
places you need to visit because it's so wonderful and different,
and I'm specifically referring to the **Duc de Morny Library**
where you can order a drink in an exquisite ornate library with
some 3,000 books from the period. There's an original wood-
burning fireplace. Try to get a chair by it in winter. It opens to
the public (that would be you and me) at 5 pm. Take in the
ornate décor, coffered ceilings, the herringbone parquet floors,
the dark green plush furnishings, order your drinks and ENJOY!
Hotel Amenities: Complimentary Wi-Fi, flat-screen TVs and
personal butlers. Onsite posh restaurant, Japanese eatery, a great

Spa with an indoor pool. Just a 5-minute walk from the Champs-Élysées and the Grand Palais museum complex.

LA SQUARE TROUSSEAU
1 rue Antoine Vollon, Paris, +33 1 43 43 06 00
www.squaretrousseau.com
CUISINE: French; bistro
DRINKS: Full Bar
SERVING: Breakfast, Lunch, Dinner
PRICE RANGE: $$$$
ARRONDISSEMENT: 12th
This romantic getaway has been featured in several French films and is a perfect example of a French brasserie with its classic interior, zinc topped bar and giant spaceship-shaped La Victoria coffee machine. The menu is typical bistro fare. Sidewalk seating. Open until 2 a.m.

LA TOUR D'ARGENT
15 quai de la Tournelle, Paris, +33 1 43 54 23 31
www.tourdargent.com
CUISINE: French
DRINKS: Full Bar
SERVING: Lunch & Dinner; closed Sun & Mon
PRICE RANGE: $$$$
ARRONDISSEMENT: 5th
Fining dining eatery with elegant décor and delicious food. This restaurant offers Old World charm and dishes that are almost too beautiful to eat. This definitely NOT one of the trendier spots in Paris. Yes, the celebrities used to flock here, but now it's mainly an attraction for tourists. The Duck Tour d'Argent is a favorite, and has been over for over a hundred years. The recipe is exactly the same, so if you get it, you'll know how it tasted to President Franklin Roosevelt and Marlene Dietrich. (Each duck is numbered.) Large wine list is one of the glories of France, with some 400,000 bottles backing up about 14,000 selections. The formal setting, the quietly elegant service and the spectacular view overlooking Notre Dame make this a must-visit at least once in your life. It doesn't get more "French" than this.

LA VIERGE
A LA VIERGE DE LA RÉUNION
58 Rue de la Réunion, Paris, +33 1 43 67 51 15
https://www.facebook.com/La-vierge-1918603394915578/
CUISINE: Fusion/Vegetarian
DRINKS: Full Bar
SERVING: Lunch, & Dinner

PRICE RANGE: $$
ARRONDISSEMENT: 20th
This neighborhood eatery has been around since
1958, and still draws a devoted local crowd that
leaves happy after every meal. It's next to a very
historic cemetery, the **Père Lachaise Cemetery**,
where many famous people are buried. If you're
visiting Père Lachaise, then definitely drop by here
for lunch or an early dinner. You won't regret it.
There's a prix fixe menu separate from the a la carte
menu. (The prix fixe is always excellent.) Moreover,
the menu changes every day, and once when I had to
be in the 20th Arrondissement for 3 days, I came back
3 times, for 1 lunch and 2 dinners! Always different.
Favorites: Guinea fowl leg and Chickpeas with
eggplant. Nice selection of wines. Reservations
recommended.

L'ÉPICERIE BREIZH CAFÉ
111 rue Vieille du Temple, Paris, +33 1 42 71 39 44
www.breizhcafe.com
CUISINE: Deli
DRINKS: Beer & Wine
SERVING: Lunch & Dinner; closed Mon
PRICE RANGE: $$
ARRONDISSEMENT: 3rd
Beautiful deli filled with gourmet goodies from
Breton. Here you'll find everything from Bordier
butter to caramels and bonbons. The little café offers
a great menu including French classics and crepes.
Save room for one of their incredible desserts.

L'EPICURE AT HOTEL LE BRISTOL

112 rue du Faubourg Saint-Honoré, Paris, +33 1 53 43 43 00

www.lebristolparis.com

CUISINE: French, Bistros

DRINKS: Beer & Wine Only

SERVING: Brunch, Lunch, Dinner

PRICE RANGE: $$

ARRONDISSEMENT: 8th

This triple Michelin-starred gastronomic restaurant is located next to Hotel Le Bristol's French style garden. Menu favorites include: Eggs (Trout eggs & hen eggs) – a breakfast favorite, and Langoustines. The veal sweetbreads are a standout dish. Nice desserts. Make reservations and be sure to confirm or they will cancel.

LE 6 PAUL BERT
6 rue Paul Bert, Paris, 33 1 43 79 14 32
www.le6paulbert.com/en
CUISINE: Modern European
DRINKS: Full Bar
SERVING: Lunch, Dinner
PRICE RANGE: $$$
ARRONDISSEMENT: 11th

This quaint little bistro features an open kitchen and a six-seat bar. Very typical of Paris if you want a "local" feel. This spot attracts a lot of locals with an impressive menu of Parisian café-style fare expertly prepared. There's a little market in this casual and modern place. Chandeliers are made of wine bottles, carafes, flatware. Menu changes often. Great seafood dishes, particularly the octopus. Veal carpaccio is really good, as is the smoked cod salad with lemon mayonnaise. Menu favorites include: Tortellini with vegetables and roasted scallops with parsley and lemon. Tasty desserts like the lemon cannelloni with fromage blanc ice cream. Nice wine list of French wines.

LE BON GEORGES

45 rue St-Georges, Paris, +33 1 48 78 40 30
www.lebongeorges.com
CUISINE: Bistro
DRINKS: Beer & Wine
SERVING: Lunch & Dinner; Dinner only on Sun; closed Sat
PRICE RANGE: $$$
ARRONDISSEMENT: 9th

Perfect French bistro with excellent food. Visually, it has the "look" you associate in your mind with the word "bistro." A black chalkboard lists the daily menu, which changes as the seasons do, reflecting what's available. Traditional bistro items are always on the menu, however. Beef dishes are all good (the beef comes from cattle raised in Lorraine). The veggies for the most part come from a farm just a few miles outside Paris. Rabbit stewed with prunes; Rack of baby lamb; Yellow Pollock braised in butter; Roasted baby leeks. Excellent selection of cheeses. A charming sommelier is on duty to assist with wine.

LE CADORET

1 Rue Pradier, Paris, *+33 1 53 21 92 13*
https://www.facebook.com/Le-cadoret-
142920366465634/
CUISINE: French
DRINKS: Full Bar
SERVING: 8 a.m. to Midnight; Closed Sun & Mon
PRICE RANGE: $-$$
ARRONDISSEMENT: 19th
Popular eatery offering an everchanging menu of
French country-bistro classics like Roasted Chicken.
(You can't go wrong with the 3-course prix fixe lunch
here—quality is superior.) The place is small, only
about 20 tables, but quite charming. List of natural
wines and craft beers. Reservations recommended.
Favorite: Mussels in saffron bisque; Steak frites.

LE CHATEAUBRIAND

129 avenue Parmentier, Paris, +33 1 43 57 45 95
www.lechateaubriand.net
CUISINE: French, Brasseries, Modern European
DRINKS: Full Bar
SERVING: Lunch, Dinner
PRICE RANGE: $$$$
ARRONDISSEMENT: 11th
This popular (long lines) eatery from Chef Inaki
Aizpitarte offers a menu of contemporary French
cuisine. Menu changes daily. Menu favorites include:
Catfish and Iberian Pork. Inventive desserts like Ice
Rice Cream with Prune. Excellent wine selection.
First seating at 8 p.m. (By reservation only). Closed
Sunday & Monday.

LE CONSERVATOIRE DE CEDRIC CASANOVA

2 rue Sainte-Marthe, Paris, +33 9 51 31 33 34
www.latetedanslesolives.com
CUISINE: Italian
DRINKS: BYOB
SERVING: Lunch; closed Mon & Tues
PRICE RANGE: $$$
ARRONDISSEMENT: 10th
Next to a micro-grocery (La Tete dans les Olives)
serving Italian fare. Just a few seats, so you have to
book ahead.

LE DAUPHIN

131 ave Parmentier, Paris, +33 1 55 28 78 88
www.restaurantledauphin.net
CUISINE: French

DRINKS: Beer & Wine
SERVING: Lunch & Dinner, Dinner only on Sat, closed Sun & Mon
PRICE RANGE: $$$
ARRONDISSEMENT: 11th
Popular eatery with a hip young crowd nicely dressed. Has same chef as neighboring restaurant **Le Chateaubriand**—however, only serving small plates. My Favorites: Pigeon and Octopus, squid ink risotto, veal haché. Organic wine list. Get the lemon meringue pie for dessert.

LE GRAND COLBERT
2 rue Vivienne, Paris, +33 1 42 86 87 88
www.legrandcolbert.fr
CUISINE: French
DRINKS: Full Bar
SERVING: Lunch & Dinner
PRICE RANGE: $$$
ARRONDISSEMENT: 2nd
Popular eatery with excellent menu. Another plus: it's open on Sunday, when most restaurants in Paris are closed. My Favorites: Braised beef and Salmon dip, although I usually succumb to the lobster with fries. A tourist favorite because scenes from many movies were filmed here. Impressive wine list. Reservations recommended.

LE LAURENT
41 avenue Gabriel, Paris, +33 1 42 25 00 39
www.le-laurent.com/uk
CUISINE: French
DRINKS: Full Bar

SERVING: Lunch, Dinner (men: best to wear a jacket; a little dressy)
PRICE RANGE: $$$$
ARRONDISSEMENT: 8th
Located just off the Champs-Élysées in the 1842 pavilion once owned by Anglo-French financier Sir James Goldsmith, this elegant restaurant attracts the upper echelon in the business world, corporate CEOs and the like. It's really hard to beat the setting with the gardens just outside the window. It offers a menu of French cuisine with a contemporary twist. Menu favorites include: Breast of pigeon roasted in casserole and Browned Scallops. Exceptional wine cellar.

LE MESTURET
77 rue de Richelieu, Paris, +33 1 42 97 40 68
www.lemesturet.com
CUISINE: French
DRINKS: Full Bar
SERVING: Lunch & Dinner
PRICE RANGE: $$
ARRONDISSEMENT: 2nd
The reason it's so popular is because the price-to quality ratio is nicely balanced. My Favorites: Escargot and Grilled Chicken. English friendly. Expect a wait even with a reservation. Nice wine selection.

LE PETIT VENDOME
8 rue Capucines, Paris, +33 1 42 61 05 88
https://lepetitvendome.fr/fr
CUISINE: French/Sandwiches

DRINKS: Beer & Wine
SERVING: Breakfast, Lunch, Dinner; closed Sun
PRICE RANGE: $$
ARRONDISSEMENT: 2nd
In this little hole-in-the-wall you'll find authentic French cuisine (they have menus in English) but check out the daily specials for a treat. It's best for lunch. My Favorites: Blanquette de Veal and Beef Cheek stew. Great selection of sandwiches for take-away. Impressive wine selection.

LE REPAIRE DE CARTOUCHE
8 boulevard des Filles du Calvaire, Paris, +33 1 47 00 25 86
https://eater.space/repaire-de-cartouche
CUISINE: French
DRINKS: Beer & Wine
SERVING: Brunch, Lunch, Dinner
PRICE RANGE: $$$$
ARRONDISSEMENT: 11th
Marais North. This spectacular split-level bistro offers a menu of French regional cooking from the acclaimed Chef Rodolphe Paquin. Menu changes frequently. Menu favorites include: Sole-kari kid and Leg of Lamb from the Pyrenees. (In the winter, they have a lot of game dishes.) Classic wine list. Nice selection of old-fashioned desserts like baked custard. (Just like my French mother used to make.)

LE ROYAL MONCEAU

37 Avenue Hoche, Paris, +33 1 42 99 88 00

https://www.raffles.com/paris/

ARRONDISSEMENT: 8th

Designed by Philippe Starck, this 5-star luxury hotel offers beautiful art-filled suites and rooms. My main point here is **Le Bar Long**, which is dominated by the long bar with white underlighting (this is where you can sit, not the actual bar itself). Leave it to the ever-surprising Philippe Starck to come up with this novel idea. If you don't want to sit at the long white bar, there are plenty of little tables where it's cozier. I wanted to point you to a bar in a grand hotel that's not so formal, not so stuffy, not so filled with antiques. This is it. Hotel Amenities: flat-screen TVs and minibars. Some upscale suites come with cinemas, gyms, and kitchens. Room service available. Hotel features spa, infinity pool, cinema, art gallery and dining terrace. Guests can be pampered in the award-winning spa featuring pool, personal trainers, masseurs, and fitness classes. Walking distance from the Arc de Triomphe and the Champs-Elysées.

LE SERVAN
32 rue St-Maur, Paris, +33 1 55 28 51 82
www.leservan.com
CUISINE: Modern European
DRINKS: Beer & Wine
SERVING: Lunch; closed Mon & Tues
PRICE RANGE: $$$
ARRONDISSEMENT: 11th
Basic no frills eatery offering an ingredients-focused menu. Just a few stools at the bar and some wooden tables filling the rest of white-tiled room. Kitchen is behind the bar with a pass-through window. Closest thing to a Filipino eatery in Paris, as the sisters who run this place are from Asia. My Favorites: Mussels with Thai seasoning; Cuttle Fish; a delicious chicken

with roasted celery; chilled snails with tasty mayo; cockles braised in a ginger sauce.

LE SOT L'Y LAISSE
70 rue Alexandre Dumas, Paris, +33 1 40 09 79 20
www.lesotlylaisse.over-blog.com
CUISINE: Bistros
DRINKS: Beer & Wine Only
SERVING: Lunch, Dinner
PRICE RANGE: $$$$
ARRONDISSEMENT: 11th

This popular neighborhood bistro offers a menu of classic French dishes with Japanese influences. Prix-fix menus available. Menu favorites include: Canard roti - roasted duck and Roast fillet of turbot with Noilly Prat sauce. Creative dessert selection with a nice cheese platter available for those trying to avoid sugar. Reservations recommended. Closed Sunday.

LE VERRE VOLE

67 rue de Lancry, Paris, +33 1 48 03 17 34
www.leverrevole.fr
CUISINE: Bistros
DRINKS: Beer & Wine Only
SERVING: Lunch, Dinner
PRICE RANGE: $$
ARRONDISSEMENT: 10th

A favorite of hipsters, this small bistro close to Canal Stain-Martin serves great authentic French food. Impressive wine list. Menu changes daily, depending on which vegetables and fresh fish the chef finds when he goes to the market, but there's always his selection of sausages and charcuterie. Menu favorites include: Escargot and Duck with pumpkin puree. Reservations recommended.

LE VILLARET

13 rue Ternaux, Paris, +33 1 43 57 89 76
www.bistrotlessentiel.fr/le-villaret/
CUISINE: French
DRINKS: Beer & Wine
SERVING: Breakfast, Lunch, Dinner
PRICE RANGE: $$
ARRONDISSEMENT: 11th

This bistro offers an impressive French menu created by Chef Olivier Gaslain. Menu changes frequently. Menu favorites include: Sole meunière and Roasted country chicken. Creative dessert choices include: Pear Clafoutis and Grapefruit Quartet – grapefruit

sorbet, a grapefruit cake, candied grapefruit and roasted grapefruit. The wine list is just as impressive as the food. Closed Sundays.

LE VOLTAIRE
27 Quai Voltaire, Paris, +33 1 42 61 17 49
www.restaurantlevoltaire.com
CUISINE: French
DRINKS: Full Bar
SERVING: Lunch, Dinner
PRICE RANGE: $$
ARRONDISSEMENT: 7th
Located just across the river from the Louvre, this charming bistro offers a creative French menu and a very nice wine list. Many of the Parisian elite live in

the fancy homes near here in the 7th Arrondissement.
(And you'll see a lot of them dining here.)
Heavyweights in the fashion industry hang out here,
people like Anna Wintour and Karl Lagerfeld. You
can't get more cozy and classic than Le Voltaire.
Menu favorites include: Filet au Poivre and Entrecote
(ribeye). This is an elegant Old World experience
featuring a handwritten menu in French. (Good for
you to practice.) Maybe the best French fries in town,
and that's saying something.

LES ARLOTS

136 Rue du Faubourg Poissonnière, Paris, +33 1 42 *82 92 01*
facebook.com/lesarlots
CUISINE: French
DRINKS: Full Bar
SERVING: Lunch & Dinner; Closed Sun & Mon.
PRICE RANGE: $$
ARRONDISSEMENT: 10th
Small eatery near the Gare du Nord offering a menu of classic French cuisine. The prix fixe menu changes almost every day, and you can't go wrong with it. While there are items on the menu that aren't fish, the chef really works best with fish. Only a couple of dozen seats. The little bar only has one stool, and I try to arrive early in order to grab it, as I am usually alone. Favorites: Gnocchi and Octopus carpaccio. Impressive wine selection.

LES DEUX MAGOTS

6 place Saint-Germain des Prés, Paris, +33 1 45 48 55 25

www.lesdeuxmagots.fr

CUISINE: Italian/Vegetarian

DRINKS: Full Bar

SERVING: Breakfast, Lunch & Dinner

PRICE RANGE: $$$

ARRONDISSEMENT: 6th

Popular location as this was a hangout for the likes of Hemingway, Picasso, and Sartre. Impressive menu. My Favorites: Duck and Filet de Boeuf with peppercorn sauce. Great cappuccinos.

LES PAPILLES

30 rue Gay-Lussac, Paris, +33 1 43 25 20 79

www.lespapillesparis.fr

CUISINE: French

DRINKS: Beer & Wine Only

SERVING: Breakfast, Lunch, Dinner
PRICE RANGE: $$$
ARRONDISSEMENT: 5th
This popular restaurant offers a menu featuring "rustic regional cooking." Reservations recommended. Menu favorites include: Roasted chicken and Panna cotta for dessert. Nice wine list from independent vineyards. Great view from the tables on the terrace.

LUCAS CARTON
9 place de la Madeleine, Paris, +33 1 42 65 22 90
www.lucascarton.com
CUISINE: French
DRINKS: Beer & Wine
SERVING: Lunch & Dinner
PRICE RANGE: $$$$
ARRONDISSEMENT: 8th
Beautifully decorated (deco & modern) eatery. Perfect Parisian experience. Tasting menu with wine pairings is a good choice. My Favorites: Amuse Bouche and Dry aged beef sirloin. Creative desserts. Reservations necessary.

NEVA CUISINE
2 rue de Berne, Paris, +33 1 45 22 18 91
www.nevacuisineparis.com
CUISINE: Bistro
DRINKS: Beer & Wine
SERVING: Lunch, Dinner; closed Sun
PRICE RANGE: $$$
ARRONDISSEMENT: 8th

Elegant restaurant run by husband/wife team serving excellent contemporary French cuisine. My Favorites include: Gnocchi with Marjoram and Shrimp stuffed ravioli. Nice wine selection, including more small production Burgundies than you see elsewhere. Excellent desserts from house pastry chef.

PATISSERIE BOULANGERIE BLÉ SUCRÉ
7 rue Antoine Vollon, Paris, +33 1 43 40 77 73
CUISINE: Bakery
DRINKS: No Booze
SERVING: Breads, Baked Goods
PRICE RANGE: $$
ARRONDISSEMENT: 12th
This bakery is known for its perfect croissants and baguettes. Try their delicious chocolate croissant.

PIERRE GAGNAIRE
6 rue Balzac, Paris, +33 1 58 36 12 50
www.pierre-gagnaire.com
CUISINE: French
DRINKS: Beer & Wine
SERVING: Lunch & Dinner; closed Sun & Mon
PRICE RANGE: $$$$
ARRONDISSEMENT: 8th
Owner Chef Pierre Gagnaire not only greets guests but takes photos with the guests. Expect an incredible six-course experience. Food is complicated and almost every dish an art piece. One night he had a lamb dish that included more part of the animal than I'd ever seen before—the vadouvan-spiced chops, caul-wrapped loin; kidneys tossed with tamarind.

Highlights: Truffle risotto and the exquisite soufflé.
Reservations required & be sure to dress nicely.

PIERRE SANG
55 rue Oberkampf, Paris, +33 1 48 07 12 04
www.pierresangboyer.com
CUISINE: French/Pan Asian
DRINKS: Beer & Wine
SERVING: Lunch & Dinner
PRICE RANGE: $$$
ARRONDISSEMENT: 11th
Another perfect French eatery where the chef is the
owner and his food an unforgettable experience.
Choose the 6 dishes with 6 wine pairings and you
won't be disappointed. Expect a culinary experience
with a variety of ingredients and wonderful sauces.
Brick walls give the place a casual vibe. Try to get
one of the seats at the bar overlooking the kitchen.

PHILOU

12 avenue Richerand, Paris, +33 1 42 38 00 13
www.restophilou.com
CUISINE: French
DRINKS: Beer & Wine Only
SERVING: Lunch, Dinner
PRICE RANGE: $$$
ARRONDISSEMENT: 10th
Here you'll find a creative French menu with a great
selection of wines. Menu favorites include: Canard
Colvert rôti (roasted duck) and Entrecôte épaisse
(thick steak) with potatoes and mushrooms. Closed
Sunday & Monday.

RESTAURANT ASTIER

44 rue Jean-Pierre Timbaud, Paris, +33 1 43 57 16 35
www.restaurant-astier.com
CUISINE: French
DRINKS: Full Bar
SERVING: Lunch, Dinner

PRICE RANGE: $$$
ARRONDISSEMENT: 11th
This bistro serves classic French cuisine. Try the pre-fixe menu, which offers a nice selection in each category. Menu favorites include: Pan seared mackerel in a spicy tomato sauce and the Salmon. Try the massive cheese plate. Nice wine selection.

RESTAURANT GUY SAVOY
Monnaie de Paris
11 quai de Conti, Paris, +33 1 43 80 40 61
www.guysavoy.com
CUISINE: Italian/Vegetarian
DRINKS: Beer & Wine
SERVING: Lunch & Dinner, Dinner only on Sat; closed Sun & Mon
PRICE RANGE: $$$
ARRONDISSEMENT: 6th
When you pass through security into the Paris Mint you realize that you're in for a memorable experience. This is one of those long French dinners so be prepared. Menu changes often and Chef Savoy doesn't disappoint. Highlights: Oysters & caviar and Black truffle and artichoke soup. Reservations a must.

RESTAURANT LE MEURICE
228 rue de Rivoli, Paris, +33 1 44 58 10 55
www.alain-ducasse.com
CUISINE: French
DRINKS: Full Bar
SERVING: Lunch & Dinner, Dinner only on Sat & Sun
PRICE RANGE: $$$$

ARRONDISSEMENT: 1st

Ultimate high-end dining experience in one of the most glittering boites in town. You'll be hard pressed to find a more elegant dining room in all of Paris. Every dish is delicious, and the Michelin stars were awarded because of the modern way the chef interprets classic French techniques. My Favorites: Scallops and Baby vegetables steamed under rock salt; Duck with Cognac sauce; Sole glazed with lobster sauce. Hell, it doesn't really matter what you order. It'll be better than you expect. Tea service available after dinner. Sommelier on duty. As in many of the fanciest places, lunch prices are more reasonable, so you get to enjoy the superb surroundings at a less-than-murderous price.

RITZ BARS
15 place Vendome, Paris, +33 1 43 16 30 50
http://www.ritzparis.com/en-GB

There are 3 bars in the Ritz, and my advice is that you visit them all—each offers a different experience. There's the **Bar Vendome**, which is a lovely elegant airy room where you can get breakfast, lunch, afternoon tea, or dinner. The clubby dark-wooded **Bar Hemingway** was made famous by the American Nobel winning novelist back in the 1920s. Even renovated, it's still got tons of charm. The famous **Ritz Bar** is one of the landmarks in Paris. Every time you find yourself near the Ritz, slide in and have a drink, a single drink, as I do, and experience this great hotel for the price of that one drink.

RITZ HOTEL
COOKING CLASSES AT THE RITZ
15 place Vendome, Paris, +33 1 43 16 30 50
https://giftcard.ritzescoffier.com/courses/category/
A trip to Paris is hardly complete without at least walking through the magnificent lobby of the Ritz, and even better, having a drink at its iconic bar. But

they offer a series of cooking classes, from very intensive and specialized (tarts & little cakes, cooking a 'feast,' pastry class, a class on desserts, chocolate, madeleines, afternoon tea, etc.), but there's also a 3-hour class that might interest you. You book the class, come in, and they'll walk you through cooking a meal that you will finish by eating what you've cooked. An optional trip to the market (more fun than you might think) adds 1.5 hours to the experience. Check out their various courses. You might want to give someone a gift card allowing them to spend time in the kitchen of the most famous hotel in Paris. (I did the 2-hour course on making macarons—what a blast.) There's even a course for kids.

ROBERT
32 Rue de la Fontaine au Roi, Paris, +33 1 43 57 20 29
https://robert-restaurant.fr/
CUISINE: Gastropub/French
DRINKS: Full Bar
SERVING: Lunch & Dinner Tuesday-Saturday
PRICE RANGE: $$
ARRONDISSEMENT: 11th (near Place de la République)
Popular eatery with an open kitchen. Simple menu, plus a prix fixe option. (The menu items change weekly.) Favorite dishes: The Rabbit & ham terrine makes a great starter with a rich cold sauce ladled on top of it; Beef tartare is fine; and Pork with fresh peas & fava beans; Pasta with a lamb ragout. Excellent desserts. Menu of natural wines.

SEMILIA

54 rue de Seine, Paris, +33 1 43 54 34 50

www.semillaparis.com

CUISINE: French

DRINKS: Full Bar

SERVING: Lunch & Dinner

PRICE RANGE: $$$

ARRONDISSEMENT: 6th

Upscale dining in this bright bistro with a stainless steel open kitchen with an impressive menu (only available in French but waiters happy to translate). My Favorites: Lamb and Salmon. There's a creamy veal stew that's a knockout.

SEPTIME

80 rue de Charonne, Paris, +33 1 43 67 38 29

www.septime-charonne.fr

CUISINE: Modern European

DRINKS: Full Bar

SERVING: Lunch, Dinner

PRICE RANGE: $$$$

ARRONDISSEMENT: 11th

This popular eatery (book well in advance) serves contemporary French dishes with an impressive curated wine list. Menu favorites include: Line-Caught Tuna and Pigeon with beets and Morello cherries. This place features an open kitchen and caters primarily to a young hip crowd. While the food is top-notch, the "tone" of the place is much more relaxed than some of the stuffier establishments in Paris (of which there are quite a few). The owner says, "I wanted to liberate good French food from expensive hotel dining rooms," and, "The ceremony of haute cuisine has become boring." He got his wish—this place is the talk of the town. Creative desserts like the Apricot Sorbet with vanilla ricotta mousse.

In happier times

STRESA
7 rue Chambiges, Paris, +33 1 47 23 51 62
www.lestresa.com
CUISINE: European, Italian
DRINKS: Full Bar
SERVING: Lunch, Dinner
PRICE RANGE: $$$$
ARRONDISSEMENT: 8th
This popular Italian restaurant is a celebrity favorite. If you know someone is Paris, ask them to go with you when you come here. It's that "social." Here you'll find a fine dining experience with choices like

artichoke salad, salmon or beef carpaccio and specialty seafood dishes. Menu favorites include: Pennette Bemondo and Linguine Pasta Delon. Tables are hard to get because of the exclusive clientele.

TAILLEVENT
15 rue Lamenais, Paris, +33 1 44 95 15 00
www.taillevent.com
CUISINE: French
DRINKS: Beer & Wine
SERVING: Lunch & Dinner; closed Sat & Sun
PRICE RANGE: $$$$
ARRONDISSEMENT: 8th
Ultimate dining experience and pampering starts the moment you walk in the door, although the atmosphere is austere, very formal and not at all "fun." It's almost too serious for my taste, but again, this place is all about the food, which is plated so beautifully that you almost feel guilty when you eat it. The tables are spaced far apart as if to suggest that you shouldn't overhear anything said at a neighboring table. Tasting and à la carte menus. Impressive wine selection. Menus in French only. If you're worried about high prices, by all means avoid this place.

V
HOTEL VERNET
25 Rue Vernet, Paris, +33 1 44 31 98 00
https://www.hotelvernet-paris.com/
CUISINE: French
DRINKS: Full Bar
SERVING: Breakfast, Lunch, & Dinner
PRICE RANGE: $$$$
ARRONDISSEMENT: 8th
Located in the charming Vernet just off the Champs-Elysees is this beautiful restaurant offering an upscale dining experience. It's quite small for a fancy hotel restaurant, making it even more attractive. While the décor is very mid-century retro, with a jazzy carpet

and Jetson-like chairs, just look up and you'll be transported to the Belle Epoque by the strained glass backlighted ceiling that looks like a skylight—it was designed by Gustave Eiffel (yes, the same guy who did the Tower). Favorite dishes: The Sole drenched in butter; the Rabbit braised forever and stuffed with foie gras, if they have it; and the Risotto Carnaroli. I would easily succumb to their multi-course tasting menu. Presentation is everything. Impressive wine selection. If you don't want to spring for dinner, at least slip into the **Bar & Lounge at the Vernet** to take in the dazzling modern design by Jean-Michel Aberola—especially the ceiling with its Cubist take on things. He also did the whimsical rugs in both rooms.

VERJUS RESTAURANT AND WINE BAR
52 rue de Richelieu, Paris, +33 1 42 97 54 40
www.verjusparis.com
CUISINE: French
DRINKS: Beer & Wine
SERVING: Breakfast, Lunch, Dinner
PRICE RANGE: $$$
ARRONDISSEMENT: 1st
Fixed menus with a variety of choices focusing on French farm food. Great wine pairings. My Favorites: Honeydew with crème fraiche & caviar and Buttermilk fried chicken. Impressive wine selections. Reservations recommended. Casual wine bar downstairs (no reservations).

VIVANT TABLE
43 rue des Petites Ecuries, Paris, +33 9 67 49 96 26
http://vivantparis.com/#_=_
CUISINE: New French
DRINKS: Full Bar
SERVING: Lunch, Dinner
PRICE RANGE: $$$
ARRONDISSEMENT: 10th

Located in a 1903 restored apiary (where bees are kept), this unique restaurant features walls covered in hand-painted Gillardoni tiles. Chef Atsumi Sota serves modern French cuisine. Only organic French wines are served. Menu favorites include: Asparagus Risotto topped with black truffle and Poularde Racines (a seasoned deboned chicken with vegetables). Desserts choices include chocolate ganache.

WILLI'S WINE BAR

13 rue des Petits Champs, 75001 Paris, France
+33 1 42 61 05 09
www.williswinebar.com
CUISINE: French
DRINKS: Full Bar
SERVING: Dinner
PRICE RANGE: $$$
ARRONDISSEMENT: 1st

More than just a wine bar, this restaurant offers a nice menu of Chef François Yon's French classics to go with the variety of wines offered (and the wines are very good values, I might add). Menu changes daily. Menu favorites include: Grilled salmon and Lamb with Moroccan spices. Nice selection of desserts. Great dining experience.

YAM'TCHA

4 rue Sauval, Paris, +33 1 40 26 06 06
www.yamtcha.com
CUISINE: Tea Room / French-Asian
DRINKS: Beer & Wine
SERVING: Lunch & Dinner; closed Sun & Mon
PRICE RANGE: $$$$
ARRONDISSEMENT: 1st
Tiny little eatery that has appeared on the cooking
show Chef's Table. Beautiful dining room. Dishes
were a surprise but delicious. Steamed bao buns.
Impressive wine list. Reservations necessary.

YARD

6 rue de Mont-Louis, Paris, +33 1 40 09 70 30
www.yard-restaurant.com
CUISINE: French
DRINKS: Beer & Wine
SERVING: Lunch & Dinner, Dinner only on Sat,
Lunch only on Sun
PRICE RANGE: $$$
ARRONDISSEMENT: 11th
Small eatery next to Pere Lachaise offering a simple
seasonal menu, seems always to be busy with visiting
winemakers. The former construction yard (thus the
name) has an open kitchen. When it gets busy, the
Back Yard next door is open. Highlights: Mussels
steamed in cider; smoked trout with horseradish; Pork
shoulder cooked in milk; Rhubarb Panna Cotta.
Excellent wine list.

NIGHTLIFE

DID YOU FIND AN INTERESTING PLACE?
If you discover a place you think I should check out
on my next visit, drop me a line, will you? I'll
mention your name if I end up listing it.
andrewdelaplaine@mac.com

CHEZ RASPOUTINE
58 rue de Bassano, Paris, +33 1 47 20 02 90
www.raspoutine.com
ARRONDISSEMENT: 8th
This Erté-designed nightclub doesn't get going until
around 11:30. Inside the tables are for bottle service
only. This club, with a restaurant section serving
Russian food, attracts a straight conservative crowd.
Entertainment includes knife throwers and burlesque
dancers. (Save me, Jesus.) Electro-pop music. Dress
to impress as the door staff is very selective.

EXPERIMENTAL COCKTAIL CLUB
37 rue Saint-Sauveur, Paris, +33 1 45 08 88 09
www.experimentalevents.com
ARRONDISSEMENT: 2nd
Energy packed tiny hidden speakeasy serving
incredible cocktails. Live DJ plays everything from
old school American hip-hop to French hip-hop/dance
music.

L'ENTRÉE DES ARTISTES
30-32 rue Victor Massé, Paris, +33 1 45 23 11 93
www.lentreedesartistespigalle.com
ARRONDISSEMENT: 11th

Owners Fabien Lombardi and sommelier par excellence Edouard Vermynck have created a great little watering hole. Here you'll find a great combination of natural wines and aged cocktails. There's a wine list of bottles from the Courtois Sologne family and cocktails such as aged negroni, tequila-cucumber Chicharito, and the flaming Blow Me Down. Small plate menu available.

QUE DU BON
22 rue du Plateau, Paris, +33 1 42 38 18 65
No Website
ARRONDISSEMENT: 19th

Considered an institution among Parisian wine bars, this wine bistro also offers a menu of classic French fare. Impressive wine selection that regularly changes. On Monday nights, when other Paris restaurants are closed, you find a crowd of chefs and sommeliers.

SILENCIO
142 rue Montmartre, Paris, +33 1 40 13 12 33
www.silencio-club.com/en
ARRONDISSEMENT: 2nd
Located in the heart of Paris Grand boulevards district, this hip nightclub boasts an interior designed by filmmaker David Lynch. This place is a private club before midnight. At midnight the membership club opens its doors to the public. Note: Velvet rope door policy is very selective. If you get inside, you'll enjoy the sounds from some of the world's top DJs.

LE VERRE VOIE

67 rue de Lancry, Paris, +33 1 48 03 17 34
www.leverrevole.fr
ARRONDISSEMENT: 10th
A favorite of hipsters, this bare bones bistro/wine store is stocked with natural wines and offers a small menu of simple dishes. This place.
3 may have the look of a wine store but to many it's their favorite wine bar in the city.

INDEX

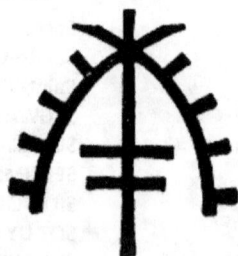

WANT 3 *FREE* THRILLERS?

Why, of course you do!

If you like these writers--

Vince Flynn, Brad Thor, Tom Clancy, James Patterson,
David Baldacci, John Grisham, Brad Meltzer, Daniel
Silva, Don DeLillo

If you like these TV series –

House of Cards, Scandal, West Wing, The Good Wife,
Madam Secretary, Designated Survivor

You'll love the **unputdownable** series about
Jack Houston St. Clair, with political intrigue, romance,
suspense.

Besides writing travel books, I've written political thrillers
for many years that have delighted hundreds of thousands
of readers. I want to introduce you to my work!
Send me an email and I'll send you a link where you can
download the first 3 books in my bestselling series,
absolutely FREE.
Mention **this book** when you email me.

andrewdelaplaine@mac.com

www.ingramcontent.com/pod-product-compliance
Lightning Source LLC
LaVergne TN
LVHW021407080426
835508LV00020B/2485